MOVING STILL

MOVING STILL

poetry

Tom McSorley

Foreword by
Atom Egoyan

ELBORO

MOVING STILL Copyright © 2023 Tom McSorley
Foreword Copyright © 2023 Atom Egoyan

All rights reserved. No part of this book may be used or reproduced in any manner whatsoever without written permission except in the case of brief quotations embodied in critical articles and reviews.

ISBN: 978-1-7379274-5-7

Published by Elboro Press

Elboro Press books may be purchased in bulk for educational, business or sales promotional use. Please address enquiries to:

office@elboropress.com

First Edition, 2023 – Second Printing

Contents

Foreword by Atom Egoyan	xi
Some Assembly Required	3
Words, Words, Words	5
Memoriam (For A.P.)	7
Elementary	9
Tracks	11
Tonight, Outside My Little Room	13
Utrecht Sliver	15
South of Sydney	17
Budapest Belvedere	19
One Train, Italy	21
Paris Haiku	23
Spanish Monument: Huesca	25
Voice	27
Uluru	29
New England Haiku Sextet	31
Distance	33
Distance, Too	35
Transience	37
Syria	39
Riga Vignette	43
Puerto Vallarta Dream	45
Berlin I: Nocturne	47
Berlin II: Ballerinas	49
Berlin III: Birthday	51
Post-Game Hotel, Hockey Tournament, Montréal	53
Guatemala City	55
Haiku: Other Russia	57
Bridging	59
LAX	61
Strathcona Hotel, Toronto: Dinner Time	63
Vancouver Taxi	65
Haiku: Sojourn NYC	67
New Brunswick Highway 8, There and Back	69
Winds of Yerevan	73
Up There Somewhere	75
Solitude At Heathrow	77

The paper is covered with indelible letters that no one spoke, that no one dictated, that have fallen there and ignite and burn and go out.

Octavio Paz,
"Toward the poem (Starting Points)" (1949)

The world is all forgetting, and the heart is a rage of directions, but your name unifies the heart, and the world is lifted into its place. Blessed is the one who waits in the traveler's heart for his turning.

Leonard Cohen,
Book of Mercy (1984)

I like to think of things as beginning not ending.

Alex Colville

Foreword

Toward the poem (Starting Points)
Octavio Paz (1949)

Toward the intro (more Starting Points)
Atom Egoyan (2023)

I've known Tom McSorley for a long time. I love the way he pronounces my name. Few have ever taken the care to emphasize the 't' in 'Atom' the way he does. But listening to Tom over the years makes me grateful that I was able to read these poems on the page and not be distracted by the comforting sound of his voice. The act of listening to a friend recite these beautiful images would buffer the gentle play between cognitive consonance and dissonance that these poems afford.

Perhaps this is that "something elusive" that Tom refers to in his poem WORDS, WORDS, WORDS. Having these words read aloud would betray the sensual pleasure of witnessing these beautifully placed letters on the page. To visually absorb the wonder of words becoming the cars of a slowly moving train thundering through nocturnal pathways. To feel so many original smaller destinations that elude. The things that shape the husks of silence. Reflecting our inward wonders. Our own dense darkness and joyous light. Each of these resonant images from the poems in this collection settle into my being and form slight scars marking remote passages. Essential signatures of being. Minor constellations of appetite. My friend marks time so faintly and yet so imprints these feelings of longing and loss with exquisite force.

Seamus Heaney once wrote of the "valency" of great poetry, of how it can give the "impression of utterance, avalanching towards vision." The poems contained in this collection never overwhelm with such catastrophic force. They describe something raw and exposed but never brutal. They describe places that have been "lived, suffered, or embraced" and are most evocative when all three feelings resonate through.

Tom's last collection was an excellent book called *Partial Clarities*. These two words perfectly define his particular voice, detailing a world with a carefully harnessed alchemy of precise measurement and gracious space. His poems are possessed of moments of great insight, always filtered through a tender and beguiling sense of longing.

They evoke, in his own words, a sense of "somnolent erotic aspiration."

Is there a better way of putting it? How can I hope to introduce a rare and unique world which the reader is about to discover so beautifully for themselves?

Now, when I imagine Tom's voice reading these poems, they are all quite perfect. And you don't need to be familiar with Tom to have this experience. You will come to know him with all the partial clarity you need to absorb his exquisite offerings.

Atom Egoyan
December 2022

Moving Still

SOME ASSEMBLY REQUIRED

A little poem
arrives upon
a new table
on an old
balcony
to announce
– or anoint –
some fresh
sense of
ritual restored.

WORDS, WORDS, WORDS

All this language
stopped up behind
some wall of silent fear;
or,
maybe
all this language
stopped is stopped
for a reason:
keeping private an
own confessional of the heart,
a place of protection and pain
to be visited,
lived, suffered, or embraced.

Not a wall at all
built with slashes of fear—
something else something
elusive and intimate,
like a quirk of dressing
or a stray hair;

these minor essential
signatures
of
being.

MEMORIAM
(for Al Purdy)

Passing through Purdy country
  blasted barns shattered trees
  soaring hawks wasted days
  a rubble of gnarled lives
    the vast witness of
      Lake Ontario.

He is gone and days remain pretty
the colours his words sketched still
fade at twilight and softly defiant
    dissolve into the sound of
      another train's solemn
          passage.

ELEMENTARY

This slow gray mist my past,
    bathing me in cold insinuations:
    you are home and you are older.
As that tall bridge over the river is a smudge in fog
      and my mother and I stride
    alongside our aching umbrellas,
      the broken streets whisper:
          you are here
            right here.

My elderly parents on this ageless river
    live for today and for yesterday.
    I maintain a shallow soft archive,
    ignoring vainly my own small now.
       The dampness insists in an
    easterly wind spun by forces far away
       gathers itself, making me
         wet and cold and
            present.

TRACKS

The old man across the aisle
has a hearing aid
and reads his newspaper
in serene silence.
His hair is gone and his suit
is baggy on his diminishing frame.

The noisy children
on this train
bring small smiles
to his lips.
He even says hello
as they burst by him.

As he closes and folds the
written world upon his lap
and sleeps a bit
before arrival,
two women behind me
mutter about misbehaviour,
how no children of theirs
would be given
such liberty.

TONIGHT, OUTSIDE MY LITTLE ROOM

Suddenly stirred
swirling snow surrenders
swept swiftly now
behind hard hurtling train,
lifted up
surprised
to settle
somewhere
else
and
distant,
as a
whisper
will return
again to
the vast
silences of night—

and
the
cold
thundering
metal moving
along
old
nocturnal
Canadian
pathways
through

shivering trees
and rocks
that take
no notice
of winter.

UTRECHT SLIVER

Olive dirt drab water
bright open faces
hoping not to close
and a slashing talk –
random rains
blow across flat earth
into the tense
happy energy
of a small
low
land.

SOUTH OF SYDNEY
(for Paul Byrnes)

Those surfers don't care —
   that southerly shouting my hair back
  and nearly lifting me off the ground
   is fuel for their waves and wetsuits and
  aquamarine spray of tenuous
     curving pathways.

No, not a care for me
  as I stand pinned to a hard
 retreating sandstone shoreline
  being shaped like a broken word
    on distant intimate
      oceans of silence.

BUDAPEST BELVEDERE

Up here on this lookout
at dusk I stand for a photo
that will turn out blurry
because you do not know my camera
but to ask me how to use it
would be
embarrassing

    flash and after flash

castles and cathedrals now closing
   slow city illumination
shapes the darkness
   staples bare trees
to the hushed night earth

down there
an old charcoal river glints
while our slipping past each other
loosens awkward goodbyes
inarticulate longings
vague
hopes
of
return.

ONE TRAIN, ITALY

Vineyards,
and I've taken the wrong train;
 that old river,
and my slow confusion.
No, I smile mutely at the attendant,
I don't want coffee
or birra or vino rosso.

I want a continent of flesh to
    cover my fragile
    floating frame;
I want the wine abandoned for
    this lonely body;
I want shutters closed
    to deepen the solitude
    of the encounter;
I want stillness in the hotel's witnesses:
    these floors and walls,
    the slack orphaned chairs,
    that dripping water which now hesitates
      out of respect,
      while the lonesome
      in other rooms
      beg for intimates on this
      long impersonal night.

"Treviso," you deliver, bemused,
    and I disembark.
I turn around
    catch the train
    going back
    to an original

   smaller destination
    that eluded me
in soft disciplined
   landscapes of
  ever yielding vines
wrapped in a skein of rails
      warmed
  under metal wheels.

PARIS HAIKU

        tourist camera
    a frail gauze of images
small faint larcenies

SPANISH MONUMENT: HUESCA

From a country
young and cold
I stand on your
hot and aged
earth before a
Civil War monument.

As the photographer
motions, I wonder
how to pose:
should I tilt my head
slightly down to
suggest humility?,
or look up
through dark trees to
the azure sky to
sketch youth and pride?

Will the baldness show?

(How many died
fighting fascism
in Huesca?)

Should I smile?

The photographer waits,
his history balanced
finely on supple shoulders,
now and then
lacerating gently.
I turn my head,

breathe the dust and blood
into my Canadian calm.
Now I am ready.

Shoot me.

VOICE

There is
another woman
with your voice,
I swear.

How she got it,
I'm not sure.

All I know
is that
when
she speaks

she shapes
the hush
of your
absence.

ULURU

Stone mirror breathes
invisible winds,
sucks water from ancient dust
and swirls my thoughts
over smooth rust contours,
against buried cosmologies
aged and new.

A mirror of all times
dreamed and lived,
reflecting nothing
but our inward wonder
at our own dense
darkness.

NEW ENGLAND HAIKU SEXTET

You sleep when we're still
   roads exhausted together
my pen cannot rest

Yogi Berra lines
Massachusetts morning light
you yield to a smile

There is too much here
   too much too soon and too fast
United States of

I dream on a desk
   some pure hard Shaker restraint
our taut supple sex

Wet passports alive
   more deep soft us this warm night
one world you and me

I observe your sleep
   tell myself your empty arms
stretch longing for me

DISTANCE

A strong
wide look
in your eyes;

my small
crippling
doubt.

DISTANCE, TOO

The sweet sad
sanctuary
of travel;

this
train
understands.

TRANSIENCE

There was a time when I envied you.

Your ease of movement,
your calibrated loneliness,
your precise imbalances,
your measured indifference:
all that intention in a
ghost of distance.

I, too, wanted to be aloof and alluring,
I wanted the solitude of the world weary,
an ache of unwanted desire pressing in on others—
obliging them to become your seducers
your champions,
your saviours.

These barren postures strike me as foolish now.

Not because they are fake, not because
they cauterize two souls, and not because
I am above my envy of you. No. I simply fear
brushing past others and leaving no traces,
no slight scars to mark
my remote passage.

SYRIA
(for Albert B.)

I close my eyes
as you trim
my mustache.

We talk of Lebanon,
where you will
return home for a
visit.

Imagining geography
I ask what country is
north of your home.

Syria,
you reply
as my lip
feels the breath of
your careful scissors.

I remember,
years ago now,
a young Syrian
woman washing
my soft thinning hair
in another salon

like this one.

Do you know her?
I ask after
you wipe away the
tiny cuttings
from my mouth.
She died last Friday,
your mouth says.
She was twenty-nine
and had brain cancer.
Her name was
Maïsa.

I say
how terrible;
you say
life is a gift from god.

I look
into your mirror
as you present
the back of
my head,
a ritual that
concludes
our monthly
meetings.

I thank you.

I pay you.

I say bon voyage.

And we agree
to see each
other again
when you return
from your Beirut,
a city south of
Syria.

RIGA VIGNETTE

The women dancing on the bar
are smiling at me and at all
who raise their faces from
the food the wine the little
intimacies of the table.

It is unusual, we all agree,
to have dancing women atop
a restaurant bar
smiling as their
neon bathed motions
take us from our meals
for a while and
return us soon enough
with grins, open eyes,
renewed appetites.

PUERTO VALLARTA DREAM

Down your crazy lanes
I stride Nordic
and alone
and yearning
for that warm
chaos which I
know
does
not
exist

but whose
suggestion glimmers
in the dusk
of your skin,
the crash of
those waves,
the tilts of
these broken sidewalks
and the strong sadness in
these your happy eyes.

BERLIN I: NOCTURNE

Through a falling
>   sky
  snow rises to
  your lips
       and
your eyes
as I recount James Joyce's "The Dead"
– which you have not read –
while on the wet
dirty distances of
this broken street,
in haunted
ashen air
strafed by
the purity of snows
          and
love's frayed silences,
we are
parting
perhaps
forever.

BERLIN II: BALLERINAS

Two men
each on one leg
each in delicate lingerie
bathe in the public
washroom sink
like Degas ballerinas.

I move past
all buttoned down cool
and foreign
listening as they
jabber joyful German
and alternate clean legs
for dirty ones.

BERLIN III: BIRTHDAY

When I tell you it's my birthday
you kiss my foreign head and smile
knowingly at the taxi driver whose
English is as bad as my German but
whose laugh seems as real as my father's.

And so we stumble to celebrate
in gypsy nightclubs
where odd hopeless ironies
encounter portraits of Elvis,
darkening floors, and the tawdry scents of
beer which has died,
and men like me
who are still alive
and marking time
only faintly.

POST-GAME HOTEL,
HOCKEY TOURNAMENT, MONTRÉAL

In a Holiday Inn Airport Hotel
along a gun metal gray highway
through some blind industrial park,
this beige basement room
calls itself 'Topaz,'
a bland impassive chamber
now host to minor
constellations of appetite,
somnolent erotic aspiration,
good female posture brittle,
landslide male abdomens in too tight shirts,
knowing talk of our children
and, less knowing,
of ourselves.

GUATEMALA CITY

Faraway runway lights
pierce smoky conical night
as our now sterile
cockpit descends
with me watching pilots
as a guest in their
workplace
lines of light under our
wheels and beyond
shacks in darkness
smudges of light here and there
suggest a city.

Later, at this bar
in a dark
dangerous place trembling
between volcanoes guns drug lords
murders for cell phones or jewelry
warnings to stay in the hotel
soldiers with machine guns
in the lobby –
at this bar
you speak to me
of surviving your
childhood's shadowy scars,
while I foolishly try to say
something that could be understood
as empathetic, but all I can do is
smear the condensation on my beer
glass into streaky partial clarity;
your warm smile reassures me
that you appreciate my attempt,

and my failure.

The next day
in bright sunshine
we are brought to the National Palace
to meet the President
and to witness
a little girl placing
a white rose into the hands of
a black stone sculpture,
this daily ritual marking
each and every consecutive day of
peace since the end of civil war.
Today is number 538, and we will be
leaving this evening, our jet's
wake turbulence sifting across
those runway lights to graze
faintly through darkening neighbourhoods
before settling along
splayed bottoms of
Guatemala volcanoes.

HAIKU: OTHER RUSSIA

naked trees sing
life glimmering in water
we watch Tarkovsky

BRIDGING

We walked in the sun
on the Brooklyn Bridge
and took pictures
to prove it,

while a dog in a basket
smiled by on his master's
bicycle:

this Bridge accepts
everybody.

LAX

Planes leap bravely
into blue sky
over blue Pacific Ocean
on their way
somewhere distant;
still others lift
curl back toward
continental destinations
in no less jeopardy
with browned terra firma
far down below.

STRATHCONA HOTEL, TORONTO: DINNER TIME

Hurricanes rage through the Caribbean.

Carly, in her white shirt and black bow tie,
extols the buffet dinner and,
bored by an empty hotel bistro,
rocks against a wall by the deserted elevator.

The all-news TV screen overloads us,
text and image and image and text,
while funky music thinly coats
transient lobby air.

VANCOUVER TAXI

He pulls over and picks me up. There are flecks of slush on my boots.

We speak of snow in Vancouver, this temporarily frosted metropolis on the Pacific coast. One must drive with care.

I give him my destination, and we pass through the night-time streets to get there. Looking up and out past the blur of buildings, I see the lights of ski hills atop Grouse Mountain, a spray of whiteness sunk deep between pitch black mountainside and that faraway dark canopy of night.

His accented English sounds Greek to my ears. He asks me to guess where he is from after I ask. Greece? No, he says, but my city is filled with Greeks.

The taxi driver is impressed by my now correct guess that his home city is Alexandria. I tell him a Greek poet I admire lived his life there. Cavafy. He nods. I am not certain that he has heard of him.

This Egyptian-Canadian is 69 years old and has lived in Vancouver since 1992. Before that, he lived in New York for awhile. He was last back in Egypt in 2014.

He pulls over and drops me off at my corner. As the red light pause ends and he begins to drive away, he waves me gently into my evening.

HAIKU: SOJOURN NYC

This small hotel room
A universe of longing
Sun on snowy trees

NEW BRUNSWICK HIGHWAY 8,
THERE AND BACK
(for John Leo McSorley and for my parents)

The flat arc of that gray road
will take us to grampy's place,
I recall thinking.

Rusted iron bridge and pocked pavement
sit in summer shimmer
as this river suggests destinations of its own.

The cigarette makes a bluish smudge
of my father's face as he
backs the car out of rest and we
trace the pathway to the road
to Fredericton, to grampy's place.

Across that bridge, river receding
and mom sleeping over the paper
folded to the crossword.

I've done this before, so often I
can conjure the whole route,
fast forward through its spaces.
Father smoking mother sleeping;
me dreaming of elsewhere.

Grampy greets his smoking son
and drowsy daughter-in-law.
His home is the smell of a pipe:
some sweet, rank, muscular atmosphere
of time, comfort, patience— the past.

Hello there, Tommy, is his pipe-scented salutation,

an old strong white spotted hand in mine; a
warmth, an undershirt visible beneath.

An entire history of Fredericton inhabits
his benign silences, unspoken archeologies.
They talk. I listen:

Names, deaths, births, sadnesses near and far and
past and present and *oh yes she was a nice person
and it really is a shame about Mel and I see they're
working on the Nashwaak bridge and it has been hot
but not too humid and the mill is doing well and
Tommy goes off to Ottawa in a few months and yes
his marks were good and he's got a job at the mill
and Aunt Aggie is moving into a home...*

The plastic bird bath is dried up and faded
out front on the speckled lawn;
two sparrows encounter disappointment.
Paper under my young fingers
Reader's Digest small pages
and the hope for articles on sex
("I Am Jane's Breast")
confront afternoon tedium.

Grampy mentions the Premier of New Brunswick
with laconic civic indignation;
father and mother nod their assent
with faint sceptical exhalations.
Crinkled cloudy cellophane rectangle jackets faded,
family photo albums lose their sway:
it is time to go.

'Well, Tommy, be good up there and work hard,' —
'I will' — 'Thanks for coming over to see me. Don't
wait too long to visit again
because I might not be here.'
Laughter. Knowing. Smiles.
A summer descending,
the ache of a screen door closing,
clink of lighter,
cigarette halo,
moaning reverse gear,
onward over another river
another bridge and a road
rewinding.

Grampy was right.
I never saw him again.
He left me his black jacknife.
Even now,
unused in my desk drawer,
it smells of his pipe.

WINDS OF YEREVAN
(for A.E.)

The winds of Yerevan
arrive at dusk
blowing our heated days away
down streets named after poets
out into distances
tumbling turbulences
in darkening hours,
shredding curtains of congestion
into pure tremulous fluid lines
of open breath vision.

UP THERE SOMEWHERE

       vapour trail
strafing blue altitudes
blown by high winds
into scalloped
spine
dissolving
drifting
from the path
of its already
faraway plane

SOLITUDE AT HEATHROW

I am a fool
writing bad
poetry in an
airport café
while the shopgirl
I imagined looking at me
during her break
leaves her shop
tossing
her hair and coat
and disappears
into the train
which carries
her home
everyday
without
me.

www.ingramcontent.com/pod-product-compliance
Lightning Source LLC
Chambersburg PA
CBHW070316120526
44590CB00017B/2699